*"My project rises from delight, not disappointment."*

— Toni Morrison

Bettmann/Corbis

# Toni Morrison

by Amy Robin Jones

## Cover Photo

Portrait of Toni Morrison
Horst Tappe/Archive Photos

**Published in the United States of America by The Child's World®, Inc.**
PO Box 326
Chanhassen, MN 55317-0326
800-599-READ
www.childsworld.com

**Product Manager** Mary Francis-DeMarois/The Creative Spark
**Designer** Robert E. Bonaker/Graphic Design & Consulting Co.
**Editorial Direction** Elizabeth Sirimarco Budd
**Contributors** Mary Berendes, Red Line Editorial, Katherine Stevenson, Ph.D.



**Library of Congress Cataloging-in-Publication Data**
Jones, Amy Robin, 1958–
Toni Morrison / by Amy Robin Jones.
p. cm.
Includes bibliographical references (p. ) and index.
ISBN 1-56766-925-5 (lib. bdg. : alk. paper)
1. Morrison, Toni—Juvenile literature. 2. Novelists, American —20th century—Biography—Juvenile literature. 3. African American women novelists—Biography—Juvenile literature. [1. Morrison, Toni. 2. Authors, American. 3. Women—Biography. 4. African Americans—Biography. 5. Nobel Prizes—Biography.] I. Title.
PS3563.O8749 Z72 2001
813'.54—dc21

00-013157

# Contents

AP Photos/Charles Rex Arbogast

Toni Morrison is one of the greatest American writers of the 20th century. "Good fiction," says Morrison, "should be beautiful, and powerful, but it should also work. It should have something in it that enlightens, something in it that opens the door and points the way."

# Growing Up in Ohio

Toni Morrison is one of the most important writers in America. But when she was young, nobody imagined that one day she would become famous. Her childhood name was Chloe Wofford. The Wofford family was poor and worked hard to earn a living. Chloe's parents, George and Ramah, had lived in the South before their children were born. But life in the South was difficult. Black people were treated badly, and **racism** was a way of life. So George and Ramah went to live in the North, in Ohio, and started their family soon after.

African Americans faced racism in Ohio, too. Even in the North, black people seldom were offered the best jobs. They did the most difficult or unpleasant work, yet they received poor pay. George Wofford was a shipyard welder. This was difficult and exhausting work, but he did it every day. Sometimes he worked at other jobs as well. He had four children to support, and money was tight.

Mr. Wofford taught his children to work hard and to take pride in their accomplishments. He told them stories about his past. Wofford never forgot life in the South. He felt that he could not trust white people because he had seen too much racism. He taught his children that racism should never be **tolerated.**

Ramah Wofford sang in the choir at church. She sang at home, too. Sometimes when she had a problem, she would sing all day, trying to solve it. Her children heard her singing first thing in the morning and each night as they fell asleep. Like her husband, Ramah would not let people **discriminate** against her children. One day, a new movie theater opened in town. Ramah went to see it. Some theaters would seat white people in the best seats and put black people in the back rows. Ramah made sure the new theater's **ushers** treated all of the customers equally. She had experienced enough **segregation** in the South.

Ramah vowed never to return to that way of life. In fact, she would never return to the South, even when her husband went there to visit family. Chloe would be **influenced** by her parents' strength throughout her life.

Ramah and George had four children. Chloe Anthony, the second, was born on February 18, 1931. Young Chloe grew up surrounded by hardworking people who had jobs and took good care of their families. Children were expected to help. Chloe grew up during a time known as the Great Depression. This was a period in U.S. history when there was little business activity. Many people could not find work. Even some rich people became poor. People who were already poor had to work even harder than before. During the Depression, Chloe learned how important it was to work hard. She remembered this later when she was famous and had more money.

When Chloe was growing up, her hometown of Lorain, Ohio, didn't have segregated neighborhoods. The town was too small and too poor to be segregated. Chloe grew up next door to white people. She went to school with all kinds of other children. Some of the children came from different countries and were just learning English. Some had physical handicaps, and others had mental handicaps. The school put these last two groups of children in separate classes. Chloe often thought about this. It seemed to her that the schools wanted to separate anyone who was different. She felt that she could have learned something from these children—and maybe they could have learned from her as well. This idea of separation and its **consequences** appears in many of the books she would write as an adult.

Chloe was the only black student in her first-grade class. She was also the only student who could already read. Chloe loved reading. As she grew older, she read the works of famous authors from all over the world. She did well in school. In high school, her Latin and English teachers encouraged her. They gave her books to read. They told her she was smart and that with hard work, she could go far. Their support helped her set goals and plan for her future.

Black River Historical Society, Lorain, Ohio

CHLOE WOFFORD WAS BORN IN LORAIN, OHIO (ABOVE), ABOUT 25 MILES WEST OF CLEVELAND. LORAIN WAS AN INDUSTRIAL TOWN. ITS CITIZENS WORKED IN STEEL MILLS, SHIPBUILDING PLANTS, AND AUTOMOBILE FACTORIES. MANY AFRICAN AMERICANS WENT TO LIVE IN OHIO, WHERE THEY COULD FIND WORK AND ESCAPE THE RACISM OF THE SOUTH.

Courtesy of the Lorain Public Library

THROUGHOUT HER SCHOOL YEARS, CHLOE WOFFORD WAS INVOLVED IN MANY ACTIVITIES. SHE LOVED READING AND BOOKS, SO SHE ENJOYED THE OPPORTUNITY TO WORK AS AN AIDE IN THE HIGH SCHOOL LIBRARY. SHE IS SHOWN HERE, SECOND FROM LEFT IN THE FIRST ROW, WITH OTHER LIBRARY AIDES.

Chloe learned a lot in school. She became a good writer and a class leader. Unfortunately, she also learned that racism was a big problem. Because she was such a good student, teachers often asked her to help others. Once a little boy from Greece needed her help. He sat beside Chloe, and she taught him. Every day they learned together, and soon they became friends. But one day, the boy wouldn't sit beside her. He wouldn't even speak to her. Chloe realized that he now understood they were different. He was white, and she was black. Other children had told him that he shouldn't be friends with her anymore. Chloe's friend had learned to be racist. She never forgot this difficult lesson.

Courtesy of the Lorain Public Library

CHLOE (CENTER) ENJOYED WRITING AND WORDS AS A HIGH SCHOOL STUDENT. SHE WORKED FOR THE SCHOOL PAPER, THE *HI-STANDARD.*

Courtesy of the Lorain Public Library

Chloe's high school activities prepared her for success in college. She was the class treasurer and a member of the National Honor Society. She also joined the yearbook staff and the drama club. Chloe is shown here at left.

# Learning on Her Own

After she graduated from high school, Chloe went to Howard University in Washington, D.C. Howard was one of the universities in the United States that was created for African Americans. She was excited to go there. Early on, she found that some people had trouble pronouncing her name, Chloe. So she took her middle name, Anthony, and shortened it to Toni. From that time on, everyone called her Toni.

At Howard, Toni studied English. She also joined a theater group, the Howard University Players. When the theater group toured, Toni went with them. Sometimes they went to the Southern states. There Toni saw for herself the life her parents had left. She learned more about racism and how it affected black people. She also realized how it affected white people. Toni decided that racism was a part of everyone's life. She believed that everyone should fight it.

Moorland-Springarn Research Center, Howard University

CHLOE GRADUATED FROM HIGH SCHOOL IN THE SPRING OF 1949. THAT FALL, SHE LEFT OHIO TO ATTEND HOWARD UNIVERSITY. WHILE AT COLLEGE, CHLOE BEGAN TO USE THE NAME "TONI."

Moorland- Springarn Research Center, Howard University

TONI'S INTEREST IN DRAMA CONTINUED INTO COLLEGE, WHERE SHE JOINED THE SCHOOL'S THEATER GROUP, THE HOWARD UNIVERSITY PLAYERS.

Toni graduated from Howard in 1953. Then she went to Cornell University in Ithaca, New York, to earn another degree. She continued to study English, especially the work of two writers, William Faulkner and Virginia Woolf. These and other writers influenced her own writing. She believed that a writer's work should be beautiful and simple.

After being a student for so long, Toni became a teacher. She went to Houston to teach at Texas Southern University. It was an exciting time. The **Civil Rights Movement** had begun. The university held a Negro History Week to honor black people. Toni realized that black history was an important part of American culture. She wanted to teach people about this idea. So in 1957, she went back to Howard University to teach.

In 1957, Toni returned to Howard University (shown at right), this time to work as a teacher.

Corbis

At Howard, Toni met people with similar interests. She met Andrew Young, later the mayor of Atlanta, Georgia. She met Stokely Carmichael (who later changed his name to Kwame Ture), leader of the Student Non-violent Coordinating Committee (SNCC). Toni also met and taught other writers, including poet Amiri Baraka and Claude Brown, author of *Manchild in the Promised Land.*

Toni was busy with her teaching and with black culture and politics. But she also was busy starting a new part of her life. She met a man named Harold Morrison, an **architect** from Jamaica. Toni was almost 30, and she thought she should get married. One day, Harold called and proposed to her. In 1958, they were married. Soon they had a little boy, whom they named Harold Ford. But Toni came to realize that being married was difficult and that she was unhappy. She felt that she was losing her independence.

To ease her unhappiness, Toni joined a writing group. The people in this group read their stories to each other. They worked to become better writers. Toni brought in a short story she had written. It was about a girl she had known when she was younger. The girl wanted blue eyes and prayed to God for them. The group liked her story. Morrison felt good about that, but she put the story aside. "I never planned to be a writer," Morrison said later, remembering that time in her life. "I was in a place where there was nobody I could talk to and have real conversations with. And I was also very unhappy. So I wrote then, for that reason."

Toni Morrison was pregnant with her second son when she decided she couldn't stay married any longer. In 1965, she divorced her husband. With one son to support and another child on the way, Morrison returned to live with her parents in Lorain, Ohio. Soon after, Slade Kevin was born. Although nervous about what the future would hold, Toni Morrison was ready to make a new start in life.

Corbis

WHILE MORRISON WAS A PROFESSOR AT HOWARD UNIVERSITY, THE CIVIL RIGHTS MOVEMENT WAS GAINING MOMENTUM. HOWARD WAS AN EXCITING PLACE TO BE. OVER THE YEARS, IT WOULD BE THE CENTER OF MANY DEMONSTRATIONS AND PROTESTS, WITH STUDENTS DEMANDING BETTER TREATMENT FOR AFRICAN AMERICANS.

# "I Am a Writer"

Morrison lived with her parents for a short time. But soon she was offered a job with Random House, an important publishing company. Her office was in Syracuse, New York. As an editor, she read books, fixed mistakes, and talked with authors about their writing. Her job was to help the publisher create the best books possible.

Morrison worked all day at her job, then went home and cooked dinner for her sons. They played together, and then she helped them with their homework. After they went to bed, she wrote. When she wrote, she was in a different world. This world was her own creation. She enjoyed being in that world and realized that she wanted to keep writing.

The people at Random House recognized that Morrison was very good at her job. In 1967, they offered her a job in New York City as a senior editor. Her **specialty** was black writers. She worked with many famous people, such as Muhammad Ali, Andrew Young, and Angela Davis. By this time, she also was trying to get her own book published.

Morrison knew how to write, and she knew what she wanted to write. But she had to work. She also had to care for her sons. With these responsibilities, it was difficult to find time to write. So she got up early each morning and wrote before her sons woke up. Sometimes she went to her writing desk in a quiet room, shut the door, and tried to write. But her sons would come and knock on the door, asking for a snack or the answer to a question. So Morrison took her work into the main room and worked with the boys around her. She learned that she could work anywhere, even in a noisy room. She looked forward to the challenge of writing every night.

Black River Historical Society, Lorain, Ohio

MORRISON WORKED AS AN EDITOR FOR RANDOM HOUSE, A WELL-KNOWN PUBLISHER, FOR 20 YEARS. WHEN SHE WASN'T WORKING, SHE TRIED TO FIND TIME TO WRITE. SOON WRITING BECAME AN IMPORTANT PART OF HER LIFE, SOMETHING SHE LOOKED FORWARD TO AND ENJOYED.

Toni Morrison still did not consider herself a writer at the time. Instead, writing was just a private interest. It made her feel good about herself. Whether or not anyone would publish her book was not the most important thing.

But publishers began to be interested in Morrison's work. The first of her books to be published was *The Bluest Eye.* This novel was actually the short story she had written for her writers' group. It is about the black community, and especially about children. Morrison had wanted to read books about black women and girls, but she couldn't find many. She had read many books by black writers, but most were about black men. So she decided she would write about the experiences of black women and girls.

*The Bluest Eye* is about a little girl named Pecola. Pecola wants blue eyes because she thinks that if she had them, she would be pretty. If she were pretty, then people would love her. Morrison based this book on memories of her hometown. She described the places and people in her novel. She changed names and mixed things up, but it was still much the way she remembered Lorain, Ohio.

*The Bluest Eye* was published in 1970, although Morrison had finished it much earlier. It took her a long time to find a publisher who would print it. The book was very sad. Some people didn't want to read it. They didn't want to know that bad things happened to children. But Morrison wrote a truthful story in a beautiful way. Many people were excited by what she had done. They had never read writing like hers. Morrison's story moved back and forth in time. Instead of one character telling a story, many different people told their own stories. Morrison described things that had never been described before.

The next book Morrison wrote was called *Sula. The Bluest Eye* is about children. *Sula,* published in 1973, is about women and their friendships. Sula is a woman who speaks her mind. In the story, the many strong women in Sula's family influence her.

David M. Budd Photography

**MORRISON PUBLISHED HER FIRST BOOK, *THE BLUEST EYE*, IN 1970. PEOPLE RECOGNIZED THAT SHE WAS A PROFOUND THINKER WHO COULD WRITE THOUGHTFULLY ABOUT AFRICAN AMERICAN ISSUES. SOON EDITORS ASKED HER TO WRITE ARTICLES FOR MAGAZINES AND NEWSPAPERS.**

When Sula grows up, she leaves town for a long time. When she comes back, the town is afraid of her. The people aren't used to a woman who lives and speaks for herself. They think women should take care of their husbands and their children. When Sula doesn't do that, the town rejects her and gossips about her. But Sula doesn't care. She makes up her mind about who she is and what she wants to do. Many readers thought the book was wonderful.

The focus of *Sula* was black women and the way they live their lives. But Morrison's next book, *Song of Solomon*, was about black men. Writing about men was a change for Morrison. She wanted to write about her father and the men she had known as a child. She watched her own sons to learn about black boys and men. In this book, Milkman Dead is a young man who travels from the North to the South. As he travels, he learns about his family. Morrison included stories from the lives of people she had known.

*Song of Solomon* was about the Civil Rights Movement and about violence. It was about black people wanting to find their roots. It was the longest book Morrison had written.

In 1977, *Song of Solomon* won the National Book Critics Circle Award and the American Academy and Institute of Arts and Letters Award. President Jimmy Carter appointed Morrison to the National Council on the Arts. Her work was receiving a great deal of attention, and she was becoming a respected author. After publishing *Song of Solomon,* Morrison finally began to consider herself a writer. Earlier, she had described herself as an editor who also wrote. But now she believed she was truly a writer.

Morrison's next book, *Tar Baby,* was very complicated. Again Morrison wrote about black people, but this book had white people in it, too. Published in 1981, *Tar Baby* is about white and black people and how they behave with each other. It is set in both the United States and the Caribbean. It is about rich people and poor people, black people and white people. The main character is a young African American woman, Jadine, who is a rich fashion model. She falls in love with a young man who has no money. Both are staying with white people who have money but are unhappy. Morrison wanted to write about how race separates people, but how money can separate them as well. She also wanted to write about how black people sometimes separate themselves from other blacks. Morrison wanted to explore what happened when black people from different backgrounds came together.

Morrison's life was full during this time. She edited, she taught, she took care of her sons, and she wrote. She lived like this for many years. In 1983, Morrison finally left her position as an editor at Random House. She had finally had enough of working on other people's books. She was ready to **concentrate** on teaching and writing.

After writing novels for so long, Morrison wrote a play. She was very angry about a murder that had happened in the South. *Dreaming Emmett* is about Emmett Till, a 14-year-old boy killed by white racists in 1955.

Till was accused of whistling at a white woman. In Morrison's play, the boy comes back to life and tells his side of the story. The play was performed in Albany, New York, in January of 1986.

Many of the first books Morrison wrote were **autobiographical,** based on her own experiences. Her stories weren't completely about her life, but they were about people she had known and places she had lived. Most important, they were about the lives of black people. Morrison wanted black people to be the center of her stories. She wrote about modern-day issues, events that were happening right then. But she was about to start a new novel that would be different from her other works. This new novel was set in the past. It would be one of the most important works of her career.

Morrison is shown here with her older son, Harold. For years, Morrison faced the challenge of finding time to write while working full-time and raising two boys. As the boys grew older, it became easier to dedicate more of her time to writing.

The Schomburg Center

# A Trilogy of Love

While working as an editor, Morrison had read an article about a woman named Margaret Garner. In 1851, Garner escaped a life of slavery in Kentucky and moved to Ohio. When white men came to take her and her children back to Kentucky, she tried to kill her children. She would not have them grow up as slaves. To Garner, it was better to die than to live without freedom. One of her four children died, and Margaret Garner was sent to jail.

When Morrison read this story, she knew she wanted to write about it. She didn't want to know too much about Margaret Garner. She wanted to write the story as it came to her imagination. But she did a lot of research on slavery. She read about how millions of black people had died during the time of slavery. They did not die of old age. They died because they were treated so badly. They died in the boats that brought them from Africa. They died of abuse and torture while they were slaves in America.

Morrison put the terrible things she learned about slavery into her book, *Beloved.* She wanted to make sure no one ever forgot that such horror had happened in America. Slavery seemed to be hidden by a national **amnesia,** in which people had forgotten part of the past. Morrison felt that people had tried to forget slavery. Sometimes people couldn't remember or believe how bad that time had really been. As Morrison put it, "Somebody forgot to tell somebody something." When children in schools were taught about slavery, they weren't told everything. People wanted to forget that the United States, the land of the free, had actually been built on the labor of slaves.

In *Beloved,* a woman named Sethe tries to kill her children before they are taken back to slavery. She does kill one daughter. This daughter comes back as a ghost named Beloved. Morrison grew up listening to ghost stories. She remembered her father telling the most spine-tingling stories of all. But *Beloved* isn't a scary ghost story.

Culver Pictures

THE TRAGIC STORY OF MARGARET GARNER INSPIRED MORRISON TO WRITE HER BOOK *BELOVED*. GARNER (SHOWN AT RIGHT IN THE ENGRAVING ABOVE) DID NOT WANT HER CHILDREN TO LIVE THEIR LIVES AS SLAVES, SO SHE TRIED TO KILL THEM. MORRISON WANTED TO FIND A WAY TO TELL THIS TERRIBLE TALE TO THE WORLD.

*Beloved* is about the ghosts of all black people who lost their freedom and their lives. Sethe's daughter Beloved represents all of these people.

*Beloved* won the Pulitzer Prize for literature in 1988. The Pulitzer Prize is awarded for outstanding literary achievement. It is one of the most important awards a writer in the United States can receive.

*Beloved* also was made into a movie by Oprah Winfrey and Jonathan Demme, a well-known director. Morrison was pleased with the movie, but she wanted people to keep reading books rather than just seeing movies.

With the success of her novels, Morrison devoted much of her time to writing. But she still taught as well.

MORRISON DEDICATED HER BOOK *BELOVED* TO "SIXTY MILLION AND MORE." THIS WAS THE NUMBER OF AFRICAN AMERICANS THAT MANY HISTORIANS BELIEVE DIED DURING MORE THAN 200 YEARS OF SLAVERY IN AMERICA. "THOSE 60 MILLION ARE PEOPLE WHO DIDN'T MAKE IT FROM THERE TO HERE AND THROUGH," SHE SAID. "SOME PEOPLE TOLD ME 40 MILLION, BUT I ALSO HEARD 60 MILLION, AND I DIDN'T WANT TO LEAVE ANYBODY OUT."

David M. Budd Photography

Morrison taught at many schools over the years, including Yale University, colleges in New York State, and the University of California at Berkeley. In 1989, she joined the faculty at Princeton University in New Jersey. At about that time, she began writing a new book, *Jazz.*

*Jazz* is about life in Harlem, a part of New York City where many African Americans live. The novel takes place in the 1920s, a time when jazz became a popular and important form of music. Morrison even tried to make the book sound like jazz. Jazz musicians often **improvise,** making up the music as they go along. Often they don't know where the music will go. Morrison tried to do the same thing when she wrote. She started the story even though she wasn't sure where it would go. The book was about how people love each other. Morrison felt that writing about love was important.

She ended up writing a **trilogy,** a series of three books, about love. *Beloved* was the first book, *Jazz* was the second, and *Paradise* was the third. In each book, she concentrated on how people love. People can love too much, Morrison felt. In *Beloved,* love was sometimes overpowering. In *Jazz,* love cured bad things in life. And in *Paradise,* love was confusing and uncertain.

In *Paradise,* Morrison tried to show how African Americans experience life, love, and racism. The story is set in an Oklahoma community of black people who settled there in the 1870s. They separated themselves from other people, both black and white. Their community, called Paradise, is a place where life is supposed to be perfect. But Morrison is not comfortable with her characters' idea of paradise. She sees that for them, paradise exists only when other people are **excluded**—when people who are different are kept out. Typically, white people have excluded black people. In this novel, Morrison wonders what would happen if black people **isolated** themselves from the rest of the world. They would have to keep out both white people and black people who didn't agree with their lifestyle. Would they form a sort of paradise?

© Timothy Greenfield-Sanders

MORRISON WROTE ABOUT A BLACK COMMUNITY IN *PARADISE*, BUT SHE DID NOT TELL THE READER WHAT RACE THE PEOPLE WERE. SHE LEFT IT UP TO THE READER TO DECIDE. MORRISON WANTED READERS TO THINK ABOUT WHAT MAKES A PERSON A MEMBER OF A RACE. SHE ALSO WANTED READERS TO THINK ABOUT HOW THEY RESPOND TO DIFFERENT RACES.

Morrison remembered that when she was a child in school, some children were separated from the rest. She had always believed that separating people was a bad idea. This belief shows up again in *Paradise.* The story is about how the changing world affects isolated people. The people in her novel experience war, the Great Depression, the Civil Rights Movement—all sorts of events. But because they live away from everyone else, they see these events and the world in a different way.

Courtesy of Princeton University

**In 1989, Morrison began teaching at Princeton University, one of the most respected colleges in the United States.**

# A Larger World

Even before *Paradise* was published, Toni Morrison received the highest international honor a writer can receive. In 1993, she received the Nobel Prize in Literature. Toni Morrison was the first black woman ever to receive this award. She received prize money of about $800,000. But even more important, she was recognized by the world as a great writer.

Morrison was proud, but she had a lot to do to prepare. She had to write a speech and dress up. She made a joke about it, saying, "If you're going to keep giving prizes to women—and I hope you do—you're going to have to give us more warning. Men can rent tuxedos. I have to get shoes, I have to get a dress." The speech she needed to write was an important one. She worked on it carefully. In her speech, she talked about language and how important it was. She said that as human beings, we all must die. But language lives on. To Morrison, language is how people look at their lives, the past, the present, and the future.

Some people have criticized Morrison's writing. Some think her work is too political. They feel that she concentrates too much on black life and should write about the rest of the world. Others have said that her novels are too sad or too violent. Others think she writes in a complicated style that many people can't understand. They feel she uses too many words that not everyone understands. Such criticisms bother Morrison for a little while. Bad reviews that are written poorly bother her a little bit longer. But Morrison says that no matter what, being able to laugh gets her through tough times.

Morrison continues to write. She begins writing all her books with a pen but then switches to a computer. Her stories sometimes seem to jump around. But she says that life is experienced "as the present moment, the **anticipation** of the future, and a lot of slices of the past." When she writes, she knows the beginning and the end of her story. But she doesn't always know what will happen in the middle.

Reuters/Pressen Bild/Archive Photos

TONI MORRISON IS SHOWN HERE RECEIVING THE 1993 NOBEL PRIZE IN LITERATURE FROM THE KING OF SWEDEN, CARL GUSTAV. MORRISON WAS THE FIRST BLACK WOMAN TO RECEIVE THIS AWARD.

Morrison does know that her characters have to do certain things to show readers the main idea of the story.

Some of Morrison's stories are set in the past. She reads old newspapers and magazines, using what she learns to make her stories seem more real. Morrison also reads about history and about contemporary events. The things she reads inspire her to write. Sometimes a single phrase or event inspires her to explore it further through writing.

Morrison says that the first part of writing is difficult. But **revising,** or going back to make changes, is wonderful. That's when she sees what parts of her work are good and finds ways to make them even better. Sometimes she revises for hours and ends up with fewer pages than when she started.

Morrison feels lonely when she finishes a book. She misses the characters. But then she starts thinking about a new book and new characters. She also thinks about life in America.

Morrison is concerned about racism in her country. She thinks that violent racism is still a big problem. She writes **essays** to make people think differently about life in the United States. Morrison knows people listen to her. She is careful about what she says and how she says it. But she will not be silent. She will write what she believes, and she will write to make people think.

Describing Toni Morrison is both easy and hard. She is a famous writer, but she is also a quiet, private person who likes to be at home. She is not tall, but she has a strong presence. Her silver hair is often done up in dreadlocks. She has a few very close friends. She also has a grandchild. That might be why she recently wrote a children's book with her son, Slade. The book is called *The Big Box,* and it is about freedom.

Morrison has never remarried. She likes her independence. When she isn't writing, she likes to read. She likes to garden and especially enjoys growing flowers. And she likes watching birds.

Courtesy of Princeton University

In addition to writing, Morrison is still a professor at Princeton University. Her classes are popular with students, who feel fortunate to study with a great American writer.

The people of Lorain, Ohio, are proud that Toni Morrison came from their town. The library dedicated a special room to her, calling it the Toni Morrison Reading Room. She is shown here (second from left) with several people who came to honor her achievements.

Courtesy of the Lorain Public Library

Through her writing, Toni Morrison is a person who can change how other people think and feel. Doing that means the writer must be sure of her own ideas. Morrison's writing has changed not only literature but the world itself. She has brought the black experience to the attention of all kinds of Americans. She has reminded people that black women and black children have important stories to tell. She has reminded Americans of their tragic history of slavery, something many people would like to forget.

If you asked Toni Morrison to describe herself, she might say, "I am a black woman writer, and that makes my world larger." The world of Toni Morrison has made people laugh and cry, think and change—and that is a writer's job.

TIME
TEENS ON DEATH ROW
YELLOWSTONE'S WOLF WAR
The Sound And the Fury of Toni Morrison
With her new novel Paradise, the Nobel laureate shows that she's the Great American Storyteller

# Timeline

**1931** Chloe Anthony Wofford is born on February 18 in Lorain, Ohio.

**1949** Chloe graduates from Lorain High School and then enters Howard University in Washington, D.C. At Howard, she becomes known as Toni, a shortened version of her middle name.

**1953** Toni graduates from Howard University with a degree in English.

**1955** Toni receives a degree from Cornell University in Ithaca, New York. She then begins teaching at Texas Southern University in Houston.

**1957** Toni teaches in the English department at Howard University.

**1958** Toni marries a Jamaican architect named Harold Morrison.

**1961** The Morrisons' first son, Harold Ford, is born.

**1965** Toni Morrison divorces her husband and moves back to Lorain, Ohio. Her second son, Slade Kevin, is born. She is offered a job as an editor at Random House, an important publishing company. She and her sons move to Syracuse, New York.

**1967** Morrison becomes a senior editor at Random House in New York City.

**1970** *The Bluest Eye* is published.

**1973** *Sula* is published. It is later nominated for the 1975 National Book Award.

**1977** *Song of Solomon* is published and wins both the National Book Critics Circle Award and the American Academy and Institute of Arts and Letters Award. President Jimmy Carter appoints Morrison to the National Council on the Arts.

**1981** *Tar Baby* is published, and Morrison's picture appears on the cover of *Newsweek* magazine.

**1983** Morrison leaves her position at Random House to focus on writing.

**1985** Morrison writes *Dreaming Emmett,* a play about Emmett Till, a young black man killed by whites in the South.

**1987** Morrison's fifth novel, *Beloved,* is published.

**1988** *Beloved* wins the Pulitzer Prize.

**1989** Morrison becomes a professor at Princeton University.

**1992** *Jazz,* Morrison's sixth novel, is published.

**1993** Morrison receives the Nobel Prize for Literature.

**1997** *Paradise,* Morrison's seventh novel, is published. A film based on *Beloved* is released.

**1999** With her son Slade, Toni Morrison publishes *The Big Box,* her first book for children.

# Glossary

**amnesia (am-NEE-zhuh)**
Amnesia is a condition in which people lose their memory. Toni Morrison thought that too many Americans had forgotten about slavery, as if they had a kind of amnesia.

**anticipation (an-tih-sih-PAY-shun)**
Anticipation is looking forward to some future event. Morrison has pointed out that anticipation of the future is one part of how we experience life.

**architect (AR-kih-tekt)**
An architect is a person who designs houses and other buildings. Harold Morrison, Toni's husband, was an architect.

**autobiographical (ah-toh-by-uh-GRAF-ik-ull)**
An autobiographical account or story is based on the writer's own life. Many of Toni Morrison's early books were autobiographical.

**Civil Rights Movement (SIV-el RYTZ MOOV-ment)**
The Civil Rights Movement was the struggle for equal rights for African Americans in the United States during the 1950s and 1960s. Toni Morrison has written about the Civil Rights Movement.

**concentrate (KON-sen-trayt)**
When people concentrate, they work hard at something. Morrison left her job as an editor to concentrate on writing.

**consequences (KON-seh-kwen-sez)**
Consequences are the results of something. Morrison has written about the consequences of segregation—the problems that segregation can cause.

**discriminate (dis-KRIM-ih-nayt)**
When people discriminate, they treat certain people unfairly because they are different. Morrison's parents would not let people discriminate against their children because of race.

**essays (ES-sayz)**
Essays are short written works that try to teach readers and encourage them to see things in a different way. Toni Morrison writes essays about life in the United States.

**excluded (ex-KLOOD-ed)**
When someone is excluded, he or she is shut out or kept away from others. In *Paradise,* Morrison wrote about people excluding other people.

**improvise (IM-pro-vize)**
When musicians improvise, they make up music as they play. When Morrison wrote *Jazz,* she tried to improvise, just like a jazz musician.

**influenced (IN-floo-ensd)**
When people are influenced, something has had an effect on them. The attitude of Toni Morrison's parents toward racism influenced Morrison throughout her life.

# Glossary

**isolated (EYE-suh-lay-ted)**
If people are isolated, they are set apart from others. Morrison has written about how a changing world can affect people, even when they are isolated.

**racism (RAY-sih-zim)**
Racism is a negative feeling or opinion about people because of their race. Racism can be committed by individuals, large groups, or even governments.

**revising (ree-VY-zing)**
Revising something is changing it or improving it. Once Toni Morrison has written something, she enjoys revising it to make it better.

**segregation (seh-greh-GAY-shun)**
Segregation is the practice of using laws to separate people from one another. Segregation laws separated blacks and whites in the United States for many years.

**specialty (SPESH-ul-tee)**
If people have a specialty, they focus on a special kind of study or work that they do well. As an editor, Morrison's specialty was the work of black writers.

**tolerated (TOL-er-ay-ted)**
If something is tolerated, people put up with it. Morrison's parents believed that racism should not be tolerated.

**trilogy (TRIH-luh-gee)**
A trilogy is a series of three books that are connected by the same characters or theme or idea. Toni Morrison's *Beloved* was the first book in a trilogy about love.

**ushers (USH-erz)**
Ushers are people who lead others to their seats in a theater. Morrison's mother made sure a new movie theater's ushers treated black people and white people the same.

# Index

# Further Information

## Books and Magazines

Bloom, Harold (editor). *Black American Women Fiction Writers.* Philadelphia: Chelsea House, 1995.

Bloom, Harold. *Major Modern Black American Writers.* Philadelphia: Chelsea House, 1995.

Century, Douglas, and Nathan I. Huggins. *Toni Morrison* (Black Americans of Achievement). Philadelphia: Chelsea House, 1994.

Morrison, Toni, with Slade Morrison. *The Big Box.* New York: Hyperion Press, 1999.

Wilkinson, Brenda. *African American Women Writers* (Black Stars Series). New York: John Wiley & Sons, 2000.

## Web Sites

Read interviews with Toni Morrison:
http://www.salon.com/books/int/1998/02/cov_si_02int.html
http://www.amazon.com/exec/obidos/ts/feature/7651/102-7353835-2272717

Read about Morrison's Nobel Prize in Literature:
http://nobel.sdsc.edu/literature/laureates/1993/morrison-cv.html

Read biographies of Toni Morrison:
http://www.penguinputnam.com/tonimorrison/author.htm
http://www.cwrl.utexas.edu/~mmaynard/Morrison/biograph.html

Find links to more pages about Toni Morrison:
http://www.luminarium.org/contemporary/tonimorrison/

Read works by other African American authors:
http://falcon.jmu.edu/~ramseyil/afroonline.htm